Pipe Layout Helps for the Pipefitter and Welder

by C.L. Hart (1911-1993), past member of Pipefitter Local #562, St. Louis, MO

SBN 10: 0-9624197-

SBN 13: 978-0-9624

Published by Cons 53, Clinton, NC 8329—Phone 910-___-____

For current prices and information go to Pipefitter.com: http://www.pipefitter.com or call 800-462-6487.

Table of Contents

It is not the purpose of this booklet to cover the whole field of pipe fabrication, but to present information on the most commonly used and difficult fabricating problems. The tables of constants, Table I and Table II, are taken from trigonometric tables and are written so you need not be a student of trigonometry. A knowledge of simple arithmetic is the only requirement. If you need a complete trigonometry table, one is in the back of the booklet.

The explanations of the various fabricating problems have been briefly written. In most cases, examples have been given to aid in their use. I must stress the importance of accurate measurements when laying out fabrications. The time and effort consumed in verifying the accuracy of measurements, in cutting and trimming (if necessary), in rechecking measurements, etc., is more than saved in the welding operation which follows.

We have made this booklet in a size that it can be carried with you at all times. Read it carefully to familiarize yourself with its contents so that when you need information, you can find it easily.

The Wrap-around

As all pipefitters and welders know, a wrap-around is an indispensable tool for marking cuts on pipe. The wrap-around is usually cut from a sheet of gasket material. Be sure that the edges are cut straight and true.

The wrap-around, if used properly, may be used for marking circumferential cuts, mitre cuts, 90° branches, etc. When marking for a circumferential or square cut, care should be taken that the wrap-around fits snugly against the pipe at all places and that the edges are in line where one end laps over the other.

In marking for mitre cuts or shaping 90° branches, be sure that the wrap-around is never twisted or distorted; but that it is allowed to fit snugly against the pipe—as shown in Figures 1 and 2. By studying the Figures, it will be seen that

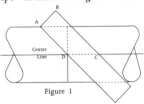

Figure 1

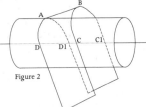

Figure 2

the wrap-around fits snugly against the pipe at points A-D-D^1-C-C^1 and a line drawn from D through A to D^1 will be straight and true.

How To Find

1. *To find length of pipe in 90° bends*, multiply radius of bend by 1.57. An alternate method is to multiply 0.01745 x degree of bend x radius. (0.01745 x 90° = 1.5702) The alternate method can be used for bends of any degree.

2. *To find end to center dimension of 45° weld fittings*, multiply diameter of fittings x 0.625. This applies only to American standard fittings having a radius equal to 1.5 times fitting diameter. (Long radius elbows)

3. *To find the pressure in pounds per square inch of a column of water*, multiply the height of the column in feet by 0.434.
   a. A gallon of water weighs 8.33 lbs. and contains 231 cubic inches.
   b. A cubic foot of water contains 7.5 gallons, 1728 cubic inches, and weighs 62.5 lbs.

4. *To find contents of cylindrical tanks*:

   Volume = 0.7854 x length x diameter^2.
   Gallons = 0.0034 x length x diameter. (If length & diameter are in inches.)
   Gallons = 5.8752 x length x diameter (If length & diameter are in feet.)

5. *To find circumference of a circle*, multiply diameter x 3.1416.

Table I

Table of constants for finding angle of turn of bends & mitred turns of any degree, up to 45°, when the dimensions for offset & travel are known. See Figure 3. Table I is also used to find cut backs for mitred turns.

To find angle of turn, divide offset "A" by travel "B".

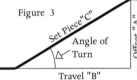

Figure 3

Example—Let "A" = 5′

Let "B"= 7′

5 ÷ 7 = 0.7142, so 0.7142 is the constant for the angle of turn. Find which constant in table is closest to 0.7142. In this case 0.7133, is the constant for 35.5°. See Table II to find length of Set piece "C".

Table I - Angles of turn

Deg	Constant	Deg	Constant	Deg	Constant	Deg	Constant
1°	0.0175	12°	0.2126	23.5°	0.4348	35°	0.7002
1.5°	0.0262	12.5°	0.2217	24°	0.4452	35.5°	0.7133
2°	0.0349	13°	0.2309	24.5°	0.4557	36°	0.7265
2.5°	0.0437	13.5°	0.2401	25°	0.4663	36.5°	0.7400
3°	0.0524	14°	0.2493	25.5°	0.4770	37°	0.7536
3.5°	0.0612	14.5°	0.2586	26°	0.4877	37.5°	0.7673
4°	0.0699	15°	0.2680	26.5°	0.4986	38°	0.7813
4.5°	0.0787	15.5°	0.2773	27°	0.5095	38.5°	0.7954
5°	0.0875	16°	0.2867	27.5°	0.5206	39°	0.8098
5.5°	0.0963	16.5°	0.2962	28°	0.5317	39.5°	0.8243
6°	0.1051	17°	0.3057	28.5°	0.5430	40°	0.8391
6.5°	0.1139	17.5°	0.3153	29°	0.5543	40.5°	0.8541
7°	0.1228	18°	0.3249	29.5°	0.5658	41°	0.8693
7.5°	0.1317	18.5°	0.3346	30°	0.5774	41.5°	0.8847
8°	0.1405	19°	0.3443	30.5°	0.5890	42°	0.9004
8.5°	0.1495	19.5°	0.3541	31°	0.6009	42.5°	0.9163
9°	0.1584	20°	0.3640	31.5°	0.6128	43°	0.9325
9.5°	0.1673	20.5°	0.3739	32°	0.6249	43.5°	0.9490
10°	0.1763	21°	0.3839	32.5°	0.6371	44°	0.9657
10.5°	0.1853	21.5°	0.3939	33°	0.6494	44.5°	0.9827
11°	0.1944	22°	0.4040	33.5°	0.6619	45°	1.0000
11.5°	0.2035	22.5°	0.4142	34°	0.6745		
		23°	0.4245	34.5°	0.6873		

Table II

This table of constants is for finding the length of Set piece "C", for any angle of turn up to 45° when offset dimension "A" and angle of turn are known. See Figure 4.

To find length of Set piece "C", multiply constant for angle of turn by offset "A".

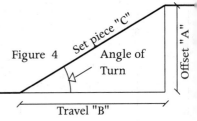

Figure 4

Example: To find length of Set Piece "C" for a 32° angle and offset "A" of 5'
(Constant for 32° = 1.8871)
1.8871 x 5' = 9.435'.
Converted to feet and regular fractional inches, 9′ 5 ¼″.
See Decimal Equivalents Table on page 34

Table II - Constants for Finding Lengths of Set Pieces

Deg	Constant	12°	4.8097	23.5°	2.5078	35°	1.7434
1°	57.2987	12.5°	4.6202	24°	2.4586	35.5°	1.7221
1.5°	38.2016	13°	4.4454	24.5°	2.4114	36°	1.7013
2°	28.6537	13.5°	4.2837	25°	2.3662	36.5°	1.6812
2.5°	22.9256	14°	4.1336	25.5°	2.3228	37°	1.6616
3°	19.1073	14.5°	3.9939	26°	2.2812	37.5°	1.6427
3.5°	16.3804	15°	3.8637	26.5°	2.2412	38°	1.6243
4°	14.3356	15.5°	3.7420	27°	2.2027	38.5°	1.6064
4.5°	12.7455	16°	3.6280	27.5°	2.1657	39°	1.5890
5°	11.4737	16.5°	3.5209	28°	2.1301	39.5°	1.5721
5.5°	10.4334	17°	3.4203	28.5°	2.0957	40°	1.5557
6°	9.5668	17.5°	3.3255	29°	2.0627	40.5°	1.5398
6.5°	8.8337	18°	3.2361	29.5°	2.0308	41°	1.5243
7°	8.2055	18.5°	3.1515	30°	2.0000	41.5°	1.5092
7.5°	7.6613	19°	3.0716	30.5°	1.9703	42°	1.4945
8°	7.1853	19.5°	2.9957	31°	1.9416	42.5°	1.4802
8.5°	6.7655	20°	2.9238	31.5°	1.9139	43°	1.4663
9°	6.3925	20.5°	2.8555	32°	1.8871	43.5°	1.4527
9.5°	6.0589	21°	2.7904	32.5°	1.8612	44°	1.4396
10°	5.7588	21.5°	2.7285	33°	1.8361	44.5°	1.4267
10.5°	5.4874	22°	2.6695	33.5°	1.8118	45°	1.4142
11°	5.2408	22.5°	2.6131	34°	1.7883		
11.5°	5.0159	23°	2.5593	34.5°	1.7655		

8

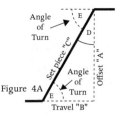

Angle of Turn

E

D

Set Piece "C"

Angle of Turn

Offset "A"

E

Travel "B"

Figure 4A

To solve for angle of turn E and length of Set piece "C" when Offset "A" is greater than Travel "B" and the angle of turn is greater than 45°. Formulas:

Travel "B" ÷ Offset "A" = constant for angle "D". Find the angle for this constant in Table I. Since angle "D" plus angle "E" equals 90°, subtract angle "D" from 90°, which will leave angle "E", the angle of turn.

Now find the constant for angle "D" in Table II. Multiply constant for angle "D" x Travel "B", which will give the length of Set piece "C". Example: Let Travel "B" = 5' and let Offset "A" = 7'.

5 ÷ 7 = 0.7142. Find constant in Table I which is closest to 0.7142. In this case, 0.7132 is the constant for Angle "D" of 35.5°.

90°-35.5°= 54.5° which is the angle of turn "E."

Constant for Angle "D" from Table II is 1.722.

1.722 x 5' = 8.610' or 8' 7⅜" which is the length of Set piece "C."

Rolling Offsets

To solve for angle of turn and length of Set piece of rolling offsets, when travel, set, and roll dimensions are given.

It is necessary to solve for the smallest angle and the hypotenuse of two triangles, the first triangle formed by the sides, set, roll and "A". See Figure 5.

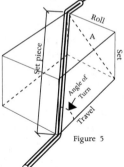

1. To solve for first triangle: Since the roll and set are given, divide the shortest side by the longest side. This will give a constant. Find this constant in Table I, which will give the degrees of the smallest angle in the triangle. Now find the constant for the smallest angle in Table II. Multiply this constant by the shortest side. The result will be the length of "A".

Figure 5

2. To solve for second triangle: Since we have solved for "A" and travel is given, divide shortest side by the longest side, and proceed as outlined for first triangle. The final result will be the length of Set piece "C". The angle formed by side marked travel and side marked Set piece "C" will be the angle of turn. The smallest angle is always opposite the shortest side. Example: Let roll = 5', Set = 3' and travel = 7'

1st triangle: Set ÷ roll or 3 ÷ 5 = 0.6000. From Table I, we find constant 0.6000 which is 31°. Find constant for 31° in Table II, which is 1.941. Multiply 1.941 x set. 1.941 x 3 = 5.823 which is length of "A".

2nd triangle: "A" ÷ travel or 5.823 ÷ 7 = 0.8313. From Table I, we find constant 0.8313 which is 39.5°. Since this angle is opposite shortest side "A", it is the angle of turn because it is formed by side travel and side Set piece "C". Find constant for angle 39.5° in Table II, which is 1.572. Multiply 1.572 by shortest side "A" or 5.823. 1.572 x 5.823 = 9.153 feet or 9' 1⅞"—the length of of Set piece "C". (See Decimal Equivalent Table on page 34.)

Method of Finding Cut Backs for Mitred Turns

The angle of cut for a mitred turn is one half the degrees of the turn. For a 30° turn, the cut angle will be 15°.

Formula for figuring cut back = Constant for angle of cut x ½ O.D. of pipe. Obtain constant for angle of cut from Table I.

Figure 6

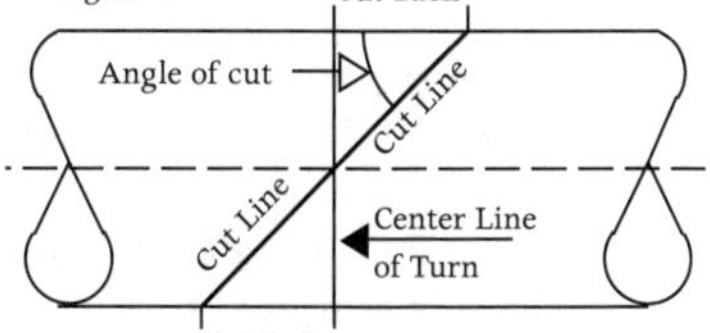

Example: Make a mitred turn of 36° on 12″ pipe. Angle of cut will be 18°, constant from Table I is 0.3249. ½ O.D. of 12″ pipe is 6⅜″ or 6.375″. 0.3249 x 6.375″ =2.071 or 2 1/16″. (See Decimal Equivalent Table on Page 33) 2 1/16″ is the cut back on each side of center line of turn. See Figure 6.

Use wraparound for marking center line and cut line.

Alternate Method of Finding Cut Back, Using Steel Square and Protractor

Set protractor on cut angle. Place point of intersection of scale and protractor on large blade of square at dimension equal to $\frac{1}{2}$ O.D. of pipe being fabricated. Where scale crosses small blade of square, dimension indicated will be cut back.

See Figure 7.

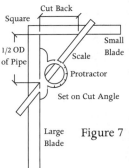

Figure 7

Methods for Laying out Pipe Bends
Standard Radius of Pipe Bends is 5 x Pipe Size

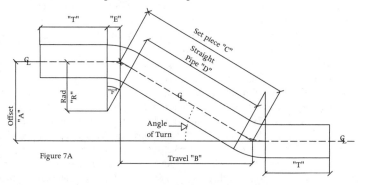

Figure 7A

Formulas: Solve for angle of turn as outlined earlier using Table I.
Solve for length of Set piece "C" as outlined using Table II.

Solve for amount of pipe in bend as follows: 0.01745 x Radius of bend x degree of bend.

Solve for End to Center of bend "E" as follows: "R" x constant for angle "F" from Table I = "E" (Angle "F" is ½ angle of turn.)

Solve for length straight pipe "D" as follows: Set piece "C" - 2 "E" = "D". Tangents "T" can be any desired length.

The best bends can be obtained on standard pipe by packing with white silica sand then heating. Care must be taken that the pipe is not heated too much. A dull, cherry red is sufficient heat.

Satisfactory bends can be made on heavier wall pipe (sch. 80 and sch. 160) without sanding. After marking pipe to be bent, start heating at one end of section and advance heat gradually toward other end. When applying bending pressure, pull slowly, and steadily. Never pull fast or in jerks.

When making an offset bend, as in Figure 7A, it is advisable to lay out and make one bend at a time. In this way you can allow for any stretching of the pipe which will take place in bending.

Making Fittings of Any Degree from 45° or 90° Long Radius Weld Ells

Constant X times degree equals B (back of ell)
Constant Y times degree equals T (throat of ell)
Example: Cut a 65° fitting from a 10" 90° L.R. weld ell.

From Table IIa, get constant X for 10" ell. 0.3556
0.3556 times 65° = $23\frac{1}{8}$". Mark this dimension on back of ell.
From Table IIa, get constant Y for 10" ell. 0.1679

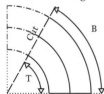

0.1679 times 65° = $10\frac{7}{8}$". Mark this dimension on throat of ell.

Use steel tape to mark dimensions and to mark cut line. Cut off square, then bevel end.

Figure 9

Table IIa

Fitting Size	Constants	
	X	Y
2	0.0752	0.0316
2½	0.0905	0.0403
3	0.1090	0.0499
4	0.1440	0.0654
5	0.1799	0.0818
6	0.2148	0.0992
8	0.2846	0.1341
10	0.3556	0.1679
12	0.4253	0.2028
14	0.4886	0.2443
16	0.5584	0.2792
18	0.6282	0.3141
20	0.698	0.349
24	0.8376	0.4188
30	1.0472	0.5236

Method of Laying Out 45° Lateral on Pipe

Divide surface of pipe into 16 spaces. See Table III for spacing. Draw longitudinal lines parallel to center axis of pipe, using soapstone for marking. Mark circumferential line around pipe, minimum distance from end of pipe, corresponding to length of longest ordinate. Number longitudinal lines, starting with #9, then each way from nine around circumference of pipe, number lines #8,

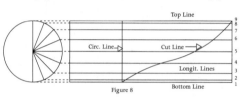

Figure 8

#7, #6, #5 etc. down to #1. There will be one #9 line, one #1 line, two #8 lines, two #7 lines, etc.

Mark off on longitudinal lines, ordinate lengths are given in Table III. (Table III on page 18) Measure carefully. Connect these points with soapstone, marking free-hand. Cut off on this line, keeping torch tip pointing to center axis of pipe at all times. After preliminary cut, bevel the end for welding. See Figure 8. Cut hole in header to fit I.D. of lateral.

Table III Ordinate lengths for 45° laterals.

Ordinate lengths for 45° laterals. I.D. of lateral to fit O.D. of header. Ordinates may be laid out on pipe or used to make patterns (templates). Most common sizes.

Pipe Size	Ordinate No. and Length				
	1	2	3	4	5
4 on 4	0	$11/32$	$1 9/32$	$2 9/16$	$3 11/16$
4 on 6	0	$9/32$	1	2	$2 15/16$
4 on 8	0	$1/4$	$15/16$	$1 13/16$	$2 15/16$
4 on 10	0	$7/32$	$7/8$	$1 3/4$	$2 5/8$
4 on 12	0	$7/32$	$13/16$	$1 5/8$	$2 7/16$
4 on 14	0	$7/32$	$13/16$	$1 9/16$	$2 3/8$
6 on 6	0	$9/16$	2	4	$5 13/16$
6 on 8	0	$1/2$	$1 11/16$	$3 5/16$	$4 3/4$
6 on 10	0	$15/32$	$1 1/2$	$2 15/16$	$4 5/16$
6 on 12	0	$7/16$	$1 7/16$	$2 13/16$	$4 1/8$

Pipe Size	Ordinate No. and Length				
	6	7	8	9	Spacing of Ordinate
4 on 4	$4\frac{1}{8}$	$4\frac{1}{8}$	$4\frac{1}{32}$	4	$\frac{7}{8}''$
4 on 6	$3\frac{1}{2}$	$3\frac{13}{16}$	4	4	$\frac{7}{8}''$
4 on 8	$3\frac{5}{16}$	$3\frac{3}{4}$	$3\frac{15}{16}$	4	$\frac{7}{8}''$
4 on 10	$3\frac{1}{4}$	$3\frac{11}{16}$	$3\frac{15}{16}$	4	$\frac{7}{8}''$
4 on 12	$3\frac{1}{8}$	$3\frac{5}{8}$	$3\frac{15}{16}$	4	$\frac{7}{8}''$
4 on 14	$3\frac{1}{8}$	$3\frac{5}{8}$	$3\frac{15}{16}$	4	$\frac{7}{8}''$
6 on 6	$6\frac{5}{16}$	$6\frac{3}{16}$	$6\frac{1}{16}$	6	$1\frac{5}{16}''$
6 on 8	$5\frac{9}{16}$	$5\frac{7}{8}$	6	6	$1\frac{5}{16}''$
6 on 10	$5\frac{1}{4}$	$5\frac{3}{4}$	$5\frac{15}{16}$	6	$1\frac{5}{16}''$
6 on 12	$5\frac{1}{16}$	$5\frac{5}{8}$	$5\frac{15}{16}$	6	$1\frac{5}{16}''$

	Ordinate No. and Length				
Pipe Size	1	2	3	4	5
6 on 14	0	$3/8$	$1 3/8$	$2 11/16$	4
8 on 8	0	$3/4$	$2 11/16$	$5 7/16$	$7 7/8$
8 on 10	0	$11/16$	$2 3/8$	$4 5/8$	$6 9/16$
8 on 12	0	$5/8$	$2 3/16$	$4 3/16$	$6 1/16$
8 on 14	0	$5/8$	$2 1/16$	4	$5 13/16$
10 on 10	0	$7/8$	$3 3/8$	$6 7/8$	$9 15/16$
10 on 12	0	$7/8$	$3 1/8$	6	$8 1/2$
10 on 14	0	$13/16$	$2 15/16$	$5 11/16$	8
12 on 12	0	$1 3/32$	$4 3/16$	$8 1/2$	$12 1/4$
12 on 14	0	$1 1/16$	$3 13/16$	$7 9/16$	$10 7/8$
14 on 14	0	$1 3/16$	$4 9/16$	$9 1/4$	$13 7/16$

Pipe Size	Ordinate No. and Length				Spacing of Ordinates
	6	7	8	9	
6 on 14	$4\,^{15}/_{16}$	$5\,^{9}/_{16}$	$5\,^{7}/_{8}$	6	$1\,^{5}/_{16}''$
8 on 8	$8\,^{1}/_{2}$	$8\,^{3}/_{8}$	$8\,^{1}/_{16}$	8	$1\,^{11}/_{16}''$
8 on 10	$7\,^{11}/_{16}$	8	$8\,^{1}/_{16}$	8	$1\,^{11}/_{16}''$
8 on 12	$7\,^{1}/_{4}$	$7\,^{13}/_{16}$	8	8	$1\,^{11}/_{16}''$
8 on 14	$7\,^{1}/_{16}$	$7\,^{3}/_{4}$	$7\,^{15}/_{16}$	8	$1\,^{11}/_{16}''$
10 on 10	$10\,^{11}/_{16}$	$10\,^{7}/_{16}$	$10\,^{1}/_{8}$	10	$2\,^{1}/_{8}''$
10 on 12	$9\,^{13}/_{16}$	$10\,^{1}/_{8}$	$10\,^{1}/_{16}$	10	$2\,^{1}/_{8}''$
10 on 14	$9\,^{1}/_{2}$	$9\,^{15}/_{16}$	10	10	$2\,^{1}/_{8}''$
12 on 12	$13\,^{1}/_{16}$	$12\,^{5}/_{8}$	$12\,^{3}/_{16}$	12	$2\,^{1}/_{2}''$
12 on 14	$12\,^{3}/_{16}$	$12\,^{5}/_{16}$	$12\,^{1}/_{8}$	12	$2\,^{1}/_{2}''$
14 on 14	$14\,^{5}/_{16}$	$13\,^{7}/_{8}$	$13\,^{1}/_{2}$	$13\,^{1}/_{4}$	$2\,^{3}/_{4}''$

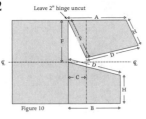

Leave 2" hinge uncut

Figure 10

Two-Piece Eccentric Reducer

A = Difference in O.D. x 2.2359
B = Difference in O.D. x 2
C = Large O.D. x 0.25
D = Answer B x 1.0606
F = ¼ Large pipe circumference
H = ¼ Small pipe circumference
See page 31 for circumferences.

This type reducer is easily made if instructions are followed carefully.

Example: Make a 6" to 4" Eccentric Reducer. First calculate values for A, B, C & D.

A = 6.625 - 4.5 = 2.125 x 2.2359 = 4.75 or 4¾"
B = 6.625 - 4.5 = 2.125 x 2 = 4.250 or 4¼"
C = 6.625 x 0.25 = 1.656 or 1 $\frac{21}{32}$"
D = 4.25 x 1.0606 = 4.50 or 4½"

Quarter the circumference of pipe & draw longitudinal lines with soapstone. Draw circumferential lines around pipe for start of reducer.

Lay out on pipe values for A, B, C, & D according to Figure 10. Make first cuts along lines D & D. Heat and shape ends to small circumference. See Figure 11. After shaping, make cuts along lines F & F. Bevel all edges. Bring down top half to match bottom half. Weld top half to bottom half. See Figure 12 for side view of finished reducer.

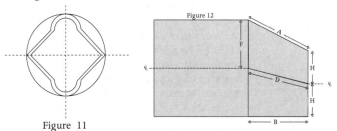

Figure 12

Figure 11

90° Branches

The most widely used method of fabrication for 90° branches is to fit the ID of the branch to the O.D. of the header. See Figure 13. Cut hole in header, the same diameter as the I.D. of branch. Keep torch tip straight so that edges of hole will he continuous with inside wall of branch. See end view Figure 14.

To determine the amount of cut back needed to shape the branch to fit the header, place a rule or square across the end of the header with the ID dimension of the branch touching the OD of the header. Now measure the distance from the midpoint of the branch to the top of the header. This will be the cut back. See Figure 15.

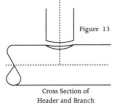

Figure 13

Cross Section of
Header and Branch

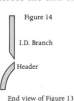

Figure 14

I.D. Branch

Header

End view of Figure 13

To layout the branch for shaping, first draw circumferential line around pipe cut back distance from the end. Draw another circumferential line around pipe ½ cut back distance from the end. Divide the surface of the pipe into 8 equal parts and draw longitudinal lines.

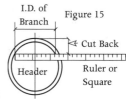

Figure 15

Number & letter intersecting points of circumferential lines & longitudinal lines as shown in Figure #16.

Using the wrap-around, draw line from A thru B to C. On opposite side of pipe draw line from F thru E to D then draw a line from A thru 1 to F. On opposite side of pipe draw line from C thru 5 to D. Cut off on this line. After cutting off, bevel for welding.

Points D, E & F are on opposite side of pipe.

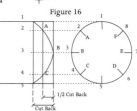

Figure 16

Method of Laying Out Hole in Header for 90° Branch

By using this method of laying out & cutting hole in header, the necessity of fitting branch to header for marking hole is eliminated, thereby cutting fit up time and effort in half.

Locate center of 90° branch on header. Through the center, draw a longitudinal line & circumferential line. The two lines cross each other at the center of the branch.

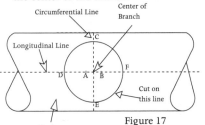

Figure 17

From Table IV, get the amount to add to ½ I.D. of branch. Measure this distance each side of center of branch on longitudinal line. Center punch these two points A & B. Set dividers to ½ I.D. of branch plus the dimension from table.

Put dividers in center punch, mark-A. Scribe line from C thru F to E. Then put dividers in mark B and scribe line from C thru D to E. Cut on this line, keeping torch pointing straight in at all times as shown in Figure 18.

Example: Cut hole in 8″ header for 8″ 90° branch. From table IV, we get a dimension of $\frac{13}{16}$″ for 8″ on 8″. Locate points A & B at $\frac{13}{16}$″ on each side of center of branch. Proceed as outlined above.

Hole will fit I.D. of branch. See Figure 17.

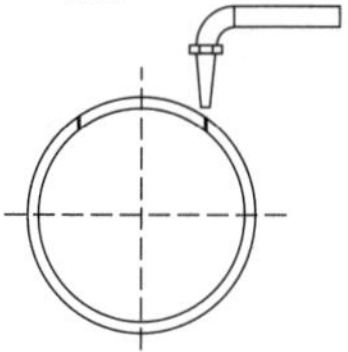

Figure 18

28

TABLE IV Adjustment for Opening on Header

Branch and Header Size	Amt to add to ½ ID of Branch	Branch and Header Size	Amt to add to ½ ID of Branch	Branch and Header Size	Amt to add to ½ ID of Branch
4 on 4	$\frac{3}{8}$	6 on 8	$\frac{1}{4}$	8 on 14	$\frac{3}{16}$
4 on 6	$\frac{3}{32}$	6 on 10	$\frac{1}{8}$	10 on 10	$1\frac{1}{32}$
4 on 8	$\frac{1}{16}$	6 on 12	$\frac{3}{32}$	10 on 12	$\frac{9}{16}$
4 on 10	$\frac{1}{16}$	6 on 14	$\frac{3}{32}$	10 on 14	$\frac{7}{16}$
4 on 12	$\frac{1}{32}$	8 on 8	$\frac{13}{16}$	12 on 12	$1\frac{5}{16}$
4 on 14	$\frac{1}{32}$	8 on 10	$\frac{3}{8}$	12 on 14	$\frac{29}{32}$
6 on 6	$\frac{17}{32}$	8 on 12	$\frac{1}{4}$	14 on 14	$1\frac{9}{16}$

Method of Layout of Bolt Holes for Flanges

= Length of chord
= Diameter of bolt circle
= Constant for each number of Divisions N
    Formula: T = D x C
= Number of bolt holes

Figure 19

Example: Make a flange with 12 bolt holes on a bolt circle diameter of 15". The constant for 12 Divisions is 0.2588. Obtain constant from Table V.

.2588 x 15= 3.882 or $3\frac{7}{8}$ ", the length of chord "T". Use dividers to lay out bolt circle diameter. Set dividers on chord length "T" and mark off hole locations on bolt circles. Drill or burn holes.

Table V-Chord Constants based on Number of Bolt Holes

N	Constant	N	Constant	N	Constant
3	0.8660	23	0.1362	43	0.0730
4	0.7071	24	0.1305	44	0.0713
5	0.5878	25	0.1253	45	0.0698
6	0.5000	26	0.1205	46	0.0682
7	0.4339	27	0.1161	47	0.0668
8	0.3827	28	0.1120	48	0.0654
9	0.3420	29	0.1081	49	0.0641
10	0.3090	30	0.1045	50	0.0628
11	0.2817	31	0.1012	51	0.0616
12	0.2588	32	0.0980	52	0.0604
13	0.2393	33	0.0951	53	0.0592
14	0.2225	34	0.0923	54	0.0581
15	0.2079	35	0.0896	55	0.0571
16	0.1951	36	0.0872	56	0.0561
17	0.1838	37	0.0848	57	0.0551
18	0.1736	38	0.0826	58	0.0541
19	0.1646	39	0.0805	59	0.0532
20	0.1564	40	0.0785	60	0.0523
21	0.1490	41	0.0766		
22	0.1423	42	0.0747		

Table VI—Pipe Circumference

NPS	O.D.	Circ.	$\frac{1}{2}$ Cir.	$\frac{1}{4}$ Cir.	$\frac{1}{8}$ Cir.	$\frac{1}{12}$ Circ.	$\frac{1}{16}$ Cir.
$\frac{1}{8}$	0.405	1.272	0.636	0.318	0.159	0.106	0.080
$\frac{1}{4}$	0.54	1.696	0.848	0.424	0.212	0.141	0.106
$\frac{3}{8}$	0.675	2.121	1.060	0.530	0.265	0.177	0.133
$\frac{1}{2}$	0.84	2.639	1.319	0.660	0.330	0.220	0.165
$\frac{3}{4}$	1.05	3.299	1.649	0.825	0.412	0.275	0.206
1	1.315	4.131	2.066	1.033	0.516	0.344	0.258
$1\frac{1}{4}$	1.66	5.215	2.608	1.304	0.652	0.435	0.326
$1\frac{1}{2}$	1.9	5.969	2.985	1.492	0.746	0.497	0.373
2	2.375	7.461	3.731	1.865	0.933	0.622	0.466
$2\frac{1}{2}$	2.875	9.032	4.516	2.258	1.129	0.753	0.565
3	3.5	10.996	5.498	2.749	1.374	0.916	0.687
4	4.5	14.137	7.069	3.534	1.767	1.178	0.884

Table VI—Pipe Circumference (concluded)

NPS	O.D.	Circ.	$\frac{1}{2}$ Circ.	$\frac{1}{4}$ Circ.	$\frac{1}{8}$ Circ.	$\frac{1}{12}$ Circ.	$\frac{1}{16}$ Circ.
5	5.563	17.477	8.738	4.369	2.185	1.456	1.092
6	6.625	20.813	10.407	5.203	2.602	1.734	1.301
8	8.625	27.096	13.548	6.774	3.387	2.258	1.694
10	10.75	33.772	16.886	8.443	4.222	2.814	2.111
12	12.75	40.055	20.028	10.014	5.007	3.338	2.503
14	14	43.982	21.991	10.996	5.498	3.665	2.749
16	16	50.265	25.133	12.566	6.283	4.189	3.142
18	18	56.549	28.274	14.137	7.069	4.712	3.534
20	20	62.832	31.416	15.708	7.854	5.236	3.927
24	24	75.398	37.699	18.850	9.425	6.283	4.712
30	30	94.248	47.124	23.562	11.781	7.854	5.890

Decimal Equivalents of an Inch in 32nds

Frac	Dec	Frac	Dec	Frac	Dec
$1/32$	0.0313	$3/8$	0.3750	$23/32$	0.7188
$1/16$	0.0625	$13/32$	0.4063	$3/4$	0.7500
$3/32$	0.0938	$7/16$	0.4375	$25/32$	0.7813
$1/8$	0.1250	$15/32$	0.4688	$13/16$	0.8125
$5/32$	0.1563	$1/2$	0.5000	$27/32$	0.8438
$3/16$	0.1875	$17/32$	0.5313	$7/8$	0.8750
$7/32$	0.2188	$9/16$	0.5625	$29/32$	0.9063
$1/4$	0.2500	$19/32$	0.5938	$15/16$	0.9375
$9/32$	0.2813	$5/8$	0.6250	$31/32$	0.9688
$5/16$	0.3125	$21/32$	0.6563	1	1.0000
$11/32$	0.3438	$11/16$	0.6875		

Decimal Equivalents of a Foot in 16ths

	0"	1"	2"	3"	4"	5"
0"	0	0.0833	0.1667	0.2500	0.3333	0.4167
1/16"	0.0052	0.0885	0.1719	0.2552	0.3385	0.4219
1/8"	0.0104	0.0938	0.1771	0.2604	0.3438	0.4271
3/16"	0.0156	0.0990	0.1823	0.2656	0.3490	0.4323
1/4"	0.0208	0.1042	0.1875	0.2708	0.3542	0.4375
5/16"	0.0260	0.1094	0.1927	0.2760	0.3594	0.4427
3/8"	0.0313	0.1146	0.1979	0.2813	0.3646	0.4479
7/16"	0.0365	0.1198	0.2031	0.2865	0.3698	0.4531
1/2"	0.0417	0.1250	0.2083	0.2917	0.3750	0.4583
9/16"	0.0469	0.1302	0.2135	0.2969	0.3802	0.4635
5/8"	0.0521	0.1354	0.2188	0.3021	0.3854	0.4688
11/16"	0.0573	0.1406	0.2240	0.3073	0.3906	0.4740
3/4"	0.0625	0.1458	0.2292	0.3125	0.3958	0.4792
13/16"	0.0677	0.1510	0.2344	0.3177	0.4010	0.4844
7/8"	0.0729	0.1563	0.2396	0.3229	0.4063	0.4896
15/16"	0.0781	0.1615	0.2448	0.3281	0.4115	0.4948

	6"	7"	8"	9"	10"	11"
0"	0.5000	0.5833	0.6667	0.7500	0.8333	0.9167
$1/16$"	0.5052	0.5885	0.6719	0.7552	0.8385	0.9219
$1/8$"	0.5104	0.5938	0.6771	0.7604	0.8438	0.9271
$3/16$"	0.5156	0.5990	0.6823	0.7656	0.8490	0.9323
$1/4$"	0.5208	0.6042	0.6875	0.7708	0.8542	0.9375
$5/16$"	0.5260	0.6094	0.6927	0.7760	0.8594	0.9427
$3/8$"	0.5313	0.6146	0.6979	0.7813	0.8646	0.9479
$7/16$"	0.5365	0.6198	0.7031	0.7865	0.8698	0.9531
$1/2$"	0.5417	0.6250	0.7083	0.7917	0.8750	0.9583
$9/16$"	0.5469	0.6302	0.7135	0.7969	0.8802	0.9635
$5/8$"	0.5521	0.6354	0.7188	0.8021	0.8854	0.9688
$11/16$"	0.5573	0.6406	0.7240	0.8073	0.8906	0.9740
$3/4$"	0.5625	0.6458	0.7292	0.8125	0.8958	0.9792
$13/16$"	0.5677	0.6510	0.7344	0.8177	0.9010	0.9844
$7/8$"	0.5729	0.6563	0.7396	0.8229	0.9063	0.9896
$15/16$"	0.5781	0.6615	0.7448	0.8281	0.9115	0.9948

American Standard Pipe Threads

Nominal Pipe Size (NPS)	Threads per inch	Drill Size	Decimal Equiv.
$\frac{1}{8}$	27	R	0.3390
$\frac{1}{4}$	18	$\frac{7}{16}$	0.4375
$\frac{3}{8}$	18	$\frac{37}{64}$	0.5781
$\frac{1}{2}$	14	$\frac{23}{32}$	0.7188
$\frac{3}{4}$	14	$\frac{59}{64}$	0.9219
1	$11\frac{1}{2}$	$1\frac{5}{32}$	1.1563
$1\frac{1}{4}$	$11\frac{1}{2}$	$1\frac{1}{2}$	1.5
$1\frac{1}{2}$	$11\frac{1}{2}$	$1\frac{47}{64}$	1.7344
2	$11\frac{1}{2}$	$2\frac{7}{32}$	2.2188

Bolt Size	Threads/Inch	Drill Size	Decimal Equiv.
$\frac{1}{4}$	20	7	0.201
$\frac{5}{16}$	18	F	0.257
$\frac{3}{8}$	16	$\frac{5}{16}$	0.3125
$\frac{7}{16}$	14	U	0.368
$\frac{1}{2}$	13	$\frac{27}{64}$	0.4219
$\frac{9}{16}$	12	$\frac{31}{64}$	0.4844
$\frac{5}{8}$	11	$\frac{17}{32}$	0.5313
$\frac{3}{4}$	10	$\frac{21}{32}$	0.6563
$\frac{7}{8}$	9	$\frac{49}{64}$	0.7656
1	8	$\frac{7}{8}$	0.875
$1\frac{1}{8}$	7	$\frac{63}{64}$	0.9844
$1\frac{1}{4}$	7	$1\frac{7}{64}$	1.1094
$1\frac{3}{8}$	6	$1\frac{7}{32}$	1.2188
$1\frac{1}{2}$	6	$1\frac{11}{32}$	1.3438

Series 15 150 lb. Flanges

Flange Size	1	$1\frac{1}{4}$	$1\frac{1}{2}$	2	$2\frac{1}{2}$	3	4	5
Flange OD	$4\frac{1}{4}$	$4\frac{5}{8}$	5	6	7	$7\frac{1}{2}$	9	10
Flange Thickness	$\frac{9}{16}$	$\frac{5}{8}$	$\frac{11}{16}$	$\frac{3}{4}$	$\frac{7}{8}$	$\frac{15}{16}$	$\frac{15}{16}$	$\frac{15}{16}$
Bolt Circle Diameter	$3\frac{1}{8}$	$3\frac{1}{2}$	$3\frac{7}{8}$	$4\frac{3}{4}$	$5\frac{1}{2}$	6	$7\frac{1}{2}$	$8\frac{1}{2}$
Number of Holes	4	4	4	4	4	4	8	8
Size of Holes	$\frac{5}{8}$	$\frac{5}{8}$	$\frac{5}{8}$	$\frac{3}{4}$	$\frac{3}{4}$	$\frac{3}{4}$	$\frac{3}{4}$	$\frac{7}{8}$
Bolt Size	$\frac{1}{2}$	$\frac{1}{2}$	$\frac{1}{2}$	$\frac{5}{8}$	$\frac{5}{8}$	$\frac{5}{8}$	$\frac{5}{8}$	$\frac{3}{4}$
Stud Length	$2\frac{1}{2}$	$2\frac{1}{2}$	$2\frac{3}{4}$	$3\frac{1}{4}$	$3\frac{1}{2}$	$3\frac{1}{2}$	$3\frac{1}{2}$	$3\frac{3}{4}$
Machine Bolt Length	2	2	$2\frac{1}{4}$	$2\frac{3}{4}$	3	3	3	3
Gasket ID	1	$1\frac{1}{4}$	$1\frac{1}{2}$	2	$2\frac{1}{2}$	3	4	5
Size OD	$2\frac{5}{8}$	3	$3\frac{3}{8}$	$4\frac{1}{8}$	$4\frac{7}{8}$	$5\frac{3}{8}$	$6\frac{7}{8}$	$7\frac{3}{4}$

6	8	10	12	14	16	18	20	24
11	13½	16	19	21	23½	25	27½	32
1	1⅛	1 3⁄16	1¼	1⅜	1 7⁄16	1 9⁄16	1 11⁄16	1⅞
9½	11¾	14¼	17	18¾	21¼	22¾	25	29½
8	8	12	12	12	16	16	20	20
⅞	⅞	1	1	1⅛	1⅛	1¼	1¼	1⅜
¾	¾	⅞	⅞	1	1	1⅛	1⅛	1¼
4	4¼	4¾	4¾	5¼	5¼	6	6¼	7
3¼	3½	4	4	4½	4½	5	5½	6
6	8	10	12	13¼	15¼	17¼	19¼	23¼
8¾	11	13⅜	16⅛	17¾	20¼	21⅝	23⅞	28¼

Series 30 300 lb. Flanges

Flange Size	1	$1\frac{1}{4}$	$1\frac{1}{2}$	2	$2\frac{1}{2}$	3	4	5
Flange OD	$4\frac{7}{8}$	$5\frac{1}{4}$	$6\frac{1}{8}$	$6\frac{1}{2}$	$7\frac{1}{2}$	$8\frac{1}{4}$	10	11
Flange Thickness	$\frac{11}{16}$	$\frac{3}{4}$	$\frac{13}{16}$	$\frac{7}{8}$	1	$1\frac{1}{8}$	$1\frac{1}{4}$	$1\frac{3}{8}$
Bolt Circle Diam.	$3\frac{1}{2}$	$3\frac{7}{8}$	$4\frac{1}{2}$	5	$5\frac{7}{8}$	$6\frac{5}{8}$	$7\frac{7}{8}$	$9\frac{1}{4}$
No. of Holes	4	4	4	8	8	8	8	8
Size of Holes	$\frac{3}{4}$	$\frac{3}{4}$	$\frac{7}{8}$	$\frac{3}{4}$	$\frac{7}{8}$	$\frac{7}{8}$	$\frac{7}{8}$	$\frac{7}{8}$
Bolt Size	$\frac{5}{8}$	$\frac{5}{8}$	$\frac{3}{4}$	$\frac{5}{8}$	$\frac{3}{4}$	$\frac{3}{4}$	$\frac{3}{4}$	$\frac{3}{4}$
Stud Length	3	$3\frac{1}{4}$	$3\frac{1}{2}$	$3\frac{1}{2}$	4	$4\frac{1}{4}$	$4\frac{1}{2}$	$4\frac{3}{4}$
Machine Bolt Lgth	$2\frac{1}{2}$	$2\frac{3}{4}$	3	3	$3\frac{1}{4}$	$3\frac{1}{2}$	$3\frac{3}{4}$	4
Gasket ID	1	$1\frac{1}{4}$	$1\frac{1}{2}$	2	$2\frac{1}{2}$	3	4	5
Size OD	$2\frac{7}{8}$	$3\frac{1}{4}$	$3\frac{3}{4}$	$4\frac{3}{8}$	$5\frac{1}{8}$	$5\frac{7}{8}$	$7\frac{1}{8}$	$8\frac{1}{2}$

6	8	10	12	14	16	18	20	24
$12\frac{1}{2}$	15	$17\frac{1}{2}$	$20\frac{1}{2}$	23	$25\frac{1}{2}$	28	$30\frac{1}{2}$	36
$1\frac{7}{16}$	$1\frac{5}{8}$	$1\frac{7}{8}$	2	$2\frac{1}{8}$	$2\frac{1}{4}$	$2\frac{3}{8}$	$2\frac{1}{2}$	$\frac{3}{4}$
$10\frac{5}{8}$	13	$15\frac{1}{4}$	$17\frac{3}{4}$	$20\frac{1}{4}$	$22\frac{1}{2}$	$24\frac{3}{4}$	27	32
12	12	16	16	20	20	24	24	24
$\frac{7}{8}$	1	$1\frac{1}{8}$	$1\frac{1}{4}$	$1\frac{1}{4}$	$1\frac{3}{8}$	$1\frac{3}{8}$	$1\frac{3}{8}$	$1\frac{5}{8}$
$\frac{3}{4}$	$\frac{7}{8}$	1	$1\frac{1}{8}$	$1\frac{1}{8}$	$1\frac{1}{4}$	$1\frac{1}{4}$	$1\frac{1}{4}$	$1\frac{1}{2}$
$4\frac{3}{4}$	$5\frac{1}{2}$	$6\frac{1}{4}$	$6\frac{3}{4}$	7	$7\frac{1}{2}$	$7\frac{3}{4}$	$8\frac{1}{4}$	$9\frac{1}{4}$
4	$4\frac{3}{4}$	$5\frac{1}{4}$	$5\frac{3}{4}$	6	$6\frac{1}{2}$	$6\frac{1}{2}$	7	8
6	8	10	12	$13\frac{1}{4}$	$15\frac{1}{4}$	17	19	23
$9\frac{7}{8}$	$12\frac{1}{8}$	$14\frac{1}{4}$	$16\frac{5}{8}$	$19\frac{1}{8}$	$21\frac{1}{4}$	$23\frac{1}{2}$	$25\frac{3}{4}$	$30\frac{1}{2}$

42

600 lb. Flanges

Flange Size	1	$1\frac{1}{4}$	$1\frac{1}{2}$	2	$2\frac{1}{2}$	3	4	5
Flange OD	$4\frac{7}{8}$	$5\frac{1}{4}$	$6\frac{1}{8}$	$6\frac{1}{2}$	$7\frac{1}{2}$	$8\frac{1}{4}$	$10\frac{3}{4}$	1
Flange Thickness	$\frac{11}{16}$	$\frac{11}{16}$	$\frac{7}{8}$	1	$1\frac{1}{8}$	$1\frac{1}{4}$	$1\frac{1}{2}$	$1\frac{3}{4}$
Bolt Circle Diam.	$3\frac{1}{2}$	$3\frac{7}{8}$	$4\frac{1}{2}$	5	$5\frac{7}{8}$	$6\frac{5}{8}$	$8\frac{1}{2}$	$10\frac{1}{2}$
Number of Holes	4	4	4	8	8	8	8	8
Size of Holes	$\frac{3}{4}$	$\frac{3}{4}$	$\frac{7}{8}$	$\frac{3}{4}$	$\frac{7}{8}$	$\frac{7}{8}$	1	$1\frac{1}{8}$
Bolt Size	$\frac{5}{8}$	$\frac{5}{8}$	$\frac{3}{4}$	$\frac{5}{8}$	$\frac{3}{4}$	$\frac{3}{4}$	$\frac{7}{8}$	
Stud Length	$3\frac{1}{2}$	$3\frac{3}{4}$	$4\frac{1}{4}$	$4\frac{1}{4}$	$4\frac{3}{4}$	5	$5\frac{3}{4}$	$6\frac{1}{2}$
Gasket ID	$1\frac{5}{16}$	$1\frac{21}{32}$	$1\frac{29}{32}$	$2\frac{3}{8}$	$2\frac{7}{8}$	$3\frac{1}{2}$	$4\frac{1}{2}$	$5\frac{9}{16}$
Size OD	$2\frac{7}{8}$	$3\frac{1}{4}$	$3\frac{3}{4}$	$4\frac{3}{8}$	$5\frac{1}{8}$	$5\frac{7}{8}$	$7\frac{5}{8}$	$9\frac{1}{2}$

Machine Bolts are not used for this class.

6	8	10	12	14	16	18	20	24
14	16½	20	22	23¾	27	29¼	32	37
1⅞	2⅛	2½	2⅝	2¾	3	3¼	3½	4
11½	13¾	17	19¼	20¾	23¾	25¾	28½	33
12	12	16	20	20	20	20	24	24
1⅛	1¼	1⅜	1⅜	1½	1⅝	1¾	1¾	2
1	1⅛	1¼	1¼	1⅜	1½	1⅝	1⅝	1⅞
6¾	7½	8½	8¾	9¼	10	10¾	11¼	13
6⅝	8⅝	10¾	12¾	14	16	18	20	24
10½	12⅝	15¾	18	19⅜	22¼	24⅛	26⅞	31⅛

Commercial Pipe Sizes and Wall Thicknesses

The following table lists the pipe sizes and wall thicknesses currently established as standard or specifically:

1. The traditional standard weight, extra strong, and double extra strong pipe.

NPS	O.D.	Sch. 5*	Sch. 10*	Sch. 20	Sch. 30	Standard	Sch. 40
$\frac{1}{8}$	0.405		0.049			0.068	0.068
$\frac{1}{4}$	0.54		0.065			0.088	0.088
$\frac{3}{8}$	0.675		0.065			0.091	0.091
$\frac{1}{2}$	0.84		0.083			0.109	0.109
$\frac{3}{4}$	1.05	0.065	0.083			0.113	0.113
1	1.315	0.065	0.109			0.133	0.133
$1\frac{1}{4}$	1.66	0.065	0.109			0.140	0.140
$1\frac{1}{2}$	1.9	0.065	0.109			0.145	0.145
2	2.375	0.065	0.109			0.154	0.154
$2\frac{1}{2}$	2.875	0.083	0.120			0.203	0.203
3	3.5	0.083	0.120			0.216	0.216

2. The pipe wall thickness schedules listed in American Standard B36.10. which are applicable to carbon steel and alloys other than stainless steels.
3. The pipe wall thickness schedules listed in American Standard B36.19. which are applicable only to stainless steels.   ASA-B36.10 and B36.19

Sch. 60	X Strong	Sch. 80	Sch. 100	Sch. 120	Sch. 140	Sch. 160	XX Strong
	0.095	0.095					
	0.119	0.119					
	0.126	0.126					
	0.147	0.147				0.187	0.294
	0.154	0.154				0.218	0.308
	0.179	0.179				0.250	0.358
	0.191	0.191				0.250	0.382
	0.2	0.2				0.281	0.400
	0.218	0.218				0.343	0.436
	0.276	0.276				0.375	0.552
	0.3	0.3				0.438	0.600

Commercial Pipe Sizes and Wall Thicknesses

NPS	O.D.	Sch. 5*	Sch. 10*	Sch. 20	Sch. 30	Standard	Sch. 40
3½	4	0.083	0.120			0.226	0.226
4	4.5	0.083	0.120			0.237	0.237
5	5.563	0.109	0.134			0.258	0.258
6	6.625	0.109	0.134			0.280	0.280
8	8.625	0.109	0.148	0.250	0.277	0.322	0.322
10	10.75	0.134	0.165	0.250	0.307	0.365	0.365
12	12.75	0.156	0.180	0.250	0.33	0.375	0.406
14	14	0.156	0.250	0.312	0.375	0.375	0.438
16	16	0.165	0.250	0.312	0.375	0.375	0.500
18	18	0.165	0.250	0.312	0.438	0.375	0.562
20	20	0.188	0.250	0.375	0.500	0.375	0.593
24	24	0.218	0.250	0.375	0.562	0.375	0.687
30	30	0.250	0.312	0.500	0.625	0.375	

Thicknesses shown above are for Schedules 5S and 10S which are available in Stainless Steel only.

Thicknesses shown are available also in Stainless steel, under the Designation Schedule 40S.

Thicknesses shown are available also in Stainless steel, under the Designation Schedule 80S.

Sch. 60	X Strong	Sch. 80	Sch. 100	Sch. 120	Sch. 140	Sch. 160	XX Strong
	0.318	0.318					
	0.337	0.337		0.438		0.531	0.674
	0.375	0.375		0.500		0.625	0.75
	0.432	0.432		0.562		0.718	0.864
0.406	0.500	0.500	0.593	0.718	0.812	0.906	0.875
0.500	0.500	0.593	0.718	0.843	1.000	1.125	
0.562	0.500	0.687	0.843	1.000	1.125	1.312	
0.593	0.500	0.75	0.937	1.093	1.250	1.406	
0.656	0.500	0.843	1.031	1.218	1.438	1.593	
0.750	0.500	0.937	1.156	1.375	1.562	1.781	
0.812	0.500	1.031	1.281	1.500	1.750	1.968	
0.968	0.500	1.281	1.531	1.812	2.062	2.343	
	0.500						

48

Trigonometry Table

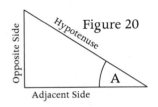

Figure 20

Formulas:

Sine of Angle "A" = Opp. Side ÷ Hypo.

Cosine of Angle "A" = Adj. Side ÷ Hypo.

Tangent of Angle "A" = Opp. Side ÷ Adj. Side

To solve for angle "A" when any two sides of a right angle triangle are given.

Example: Let adjacent side equal 48″

Let hypotenuse equal 65″

48 ÷ 65 = 0.73846 Find in trigonometry table constant which is closest to 0.73546 under column headed Cosine. The constant will be 0.7373 for 42.5°, angle "A".

To solve for other sides of right triangles when angle "A" and one side are given.

Figure 21

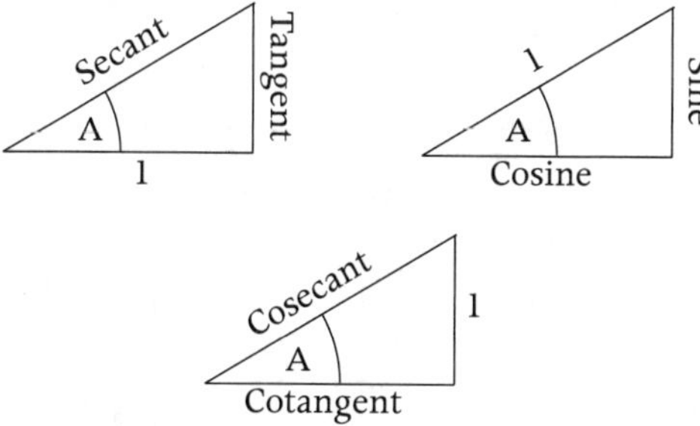

Let 1 equal given side
Let A equal given angle

Example: Find length
of hypotenuse or side
marked cosecant when
angle A equals 32° and
side 1 opposite angle
equals 24″. From trig.
tables find constant
for 32° under column
headed Cosecant, which
is 1.8871.

Multiply 1.8871 times side 1 (24″).

1.8871 x 24″ = 45.2904 or 45 ⁹⁄₃₂″

Trigonometry Table

Degree	Sine	Cosine	Tangent	Cotangent	Secant	Cosecant	
0°	0	1	0	Infinite	1	-	90°
0.5°	0.0087	1	0.0087	114.589	1	114.593	89.5°
1°	0.0175	0.9998	0.0175	57.29	1.0002	57.2987	89°
1.5°	0.0262	0.9997	0.0262	38.1885	1.0003	38.2016	88.5°
2°	0.0349	0.9994	0.0349	28.6363	1.0006	28.6537	88°
2.5°	0.0436	0.9990	0.0437	22.9038	1.0010	22.9256	87.5°
3°	0.0523	0.9986	0.0524	19.0811	1.0014	19.1073	87°
3.5°	0.061	0.9981	0.0612	16.3499	1.0019	16.3804	86.5°
4°	0.0698	0.9976	0.0699	14.3007	1.0024	14.3356	86°
4.5°	0.0785	0.9969	0.0787	12.7062	1.0031	12.7455	85.5°
5°	0.0872	0.9962	0.0875	11.4301	1.0038	11.4737	85°
5.5°	0.0958	0.9954	0.0963	10.3854	1.0046	10.4334	84.5°
6°	0.1045	0.9945	0.1051	9.5144	1.0055	9.5668	84°
6.5°	0.1132	0.9936	0.1139	8.7769	1.0065	8.8337	83.5°
7°	0.1219	0.9925	0.1228	8.1443	1.0075	8.2055	83°
	Cosine	Sine	Cotangent	Tangent	Cosecant	Secant	Degree

Trigonometry Table

Degree	Sine	Cosine	Tangent	Cotangent	Secant	Cosecant	
7.5°	0.1305	0.9914	0.1317	7.5958	1.0086	7.6613	82.5°
8°	0.1392	0.9903	0.1405	7.1154	1.0098	7.1853	82°
8.5°	0.1478	0.989	0.1495	6.6912	1.0111	6.7655	81.5°
9°	0.1564	0.9877	0.1584	6.3138	1.0125	6.3925	81°
9.5°	0.165	0.9863	0.1673	5.9758	1.0139	6.0589	80.5°
10°	0.1736	0.9848	0.1763	5.6713	1.0154	5.7588	80°
10.5°	0.1822	0.9833	0.1853	5.3955	1.017	5.4874	79.5°
11°	0.1908	0.9816	0.1944	5.1446	1.0187	5.2408	79°
11.5°	0.1994	0.9799	0.2035	4.9152	1.0205	5.0159	78.5°
12°	0.2079	0.9781	0.2126	4.7046	1.0223	4.8097	78°
12.5°	0.2164	0.9763	0.2217	4.5107	1.0243	4.6202	77.5°
13°	0.225	0.9744	0.2309	4.3315	1.0263	4.4454	77°
13.5°	0.2334	0.9724	0.2401	4.1653	1.0284	4.2837	76.5°
14°	0.2419	0.9703	0.2493	4.0108	1.0306	4.1336	76°
14.5°	0.2504	0.9681	0.2586	3.8667	1.0329	3.9939	75.5°
	Cosine	Sine	Cotangent	Tangent	Cosecant	Secant	Degree

Trigonometry Table

Degree	Sine	Cosine	Tangent	Cotangent	Secant	Cosecant	
15°	0.2588	0.9659	0.2679	3.7321	1.0353	3.8637	75°
15.5°	0.2672	0.9636	0.2773	3.6059	1.0377	3.742	74.5°
16°	0.2756	0.9613	0.2867	3.4874	1.0403	3.628	74°
16.5°	0.284	0.9588	0.2962	3.3759	1.0429	3.5209	73.5°
17°	0.2924	0.9563	0.3057	3.2709	1.0457	3.4203	73°
17.5°	0.3007	0.9537	0.3153	3.1716	1.0485	3.3255	72.5°
18°	0.309	0.9511	0.3249	3.0777	1.0515	3.2361	72°
18.5°	0.3173	0.9483	0.3346	2.9887	1.0545	3.1515	71.5°
19°	0.3256	0.9455	0.3443	2.9042	1.0576	3.0716	71°
19.5°	0.3338	0.9426	0.3541	2.8239	1.0608	2.9957	70.5°
20°	0.342	0.9397	0.364	2.7475	1.0642	2.9238	70°
20.5°	0.3502	0.9367	0.3739	2.6746	1.0676	2.8555	69.5°
21°	0.3584	0.9336	0.3839	2.6051	1.0711	2.7904	69°
21.5°	0.3665	0.9304	0.3939	2.5386	1.0748	2.7285	68.5°
22°	0.3746	0.9272	0.404	2.4751	1.0785	2.6695	68°
	Cosine	Sine	Cotangent	Tangent	Cosecant	Secant	Degree

Trigonometry Table

Degree	Sine	Cosine	Tangent	Cotangent	Secant	Cosecant	
22.5°	0.3827	0.9239	0.4142	2.4142	1.0824	2.6131	67.5°
23°	0.3907	0.9205	0.4245	2.3559	1.0864	2.5593	67°
23.5°	0.3987	0.9171	0.4348	2.2998	1.0904	2.5078	66.5°
24°	0.4067	0.9135	0.4452	2.246	1.0946	2.4586	66°
24.5°	0.4147	0.91	0.4557	2.1943	1.0989	2.4114	65.5°
25°	0.4226	0.9063	0.4663	2.1445	1.1034	2.3662	65°
25.5°	0.4305	0.9026	0.477	2.0965	1.1079	2.3228	64.5°
26°	0.4384	0.8988	0.4877	2.0503	1.1126	2.2812	64°
26.5°	0.4462	0.8949	0.4986	2.0057	1.1174	2.2412	63.5°
27°	0.454	0.891	0.5095	1.9626	1.1223	2.2027	63°
27.5°	0.4617	0.887	0.5206	1.921	1.1274	2.1657	62.5°
28°	0.4695	0.8829	0.5317	1.8807	1.1326	2.1301	62°
28.5°	0.4772	0.8788	0.543	1.8418	1.1379	2.0957	61.5°
29°	0.4848	0.8746	0.5543	1.804	1.1434	2.0627	61°
29.5°	0.4924	0.8704	0.5658	1.7675	1.149	2.0308	60.5°
	Cosine	Sine	Cotangent	Tangent	Cosecant	Secant	Degree

Trigonometry Table

Degree	Sine	Cosine	Tangent	Cotangent	Secant	Cosecant	
30°	0.5	0.866	0.5774	1.7321	1.1547	2	60°
30.5°	0.5075	0.8616	0.589	1.6977	1.1606	1.9703	59.5°
31°	0.515	0.8572	0.6009	1.6643	1.1666	1.9416	59°
31.5°	0.5225	0.8526	0.6128	1.6319	1.1728	1.9139	58.5°
32°	0.5299	0.848	0.6249	1.6003	1.1792	1.8871	58°
32.5°	0.5373	0.8434	0.6371	1.5697	1.1857	1.8612	57.5°
33°	0.5446	0.8387	0.6494	1.5399	1.1924	1.8361	57°
33.5°	0.5519	0.8339	0.6619	1.5108	1.1992	1.8118	56.5°
34°	0.5592	0.829	0.6745	1.4826	1.2062	1.7883	56°
34.5°	0.5664	0.8241	0.6873	1.455	1.2134	1.7655	55.5°
35°	0.5736	0.8192	0.7002	1.4281	1.2208	1.7434	55°
35.5°	0.5807	0.8141	0.7133	1.4019	1.2283	1.7221	54.5°
36°	0.5878	0.809	0.7265	1.3764	1.2361	1.7013	54°
36.5°	0.5948	0.8039	0.74	1.3514	1.244	1.6812	53.5°
37°	0.6018	0.7986	0.7536	1.327	1.2521	1.6616	53°
	Cosine	Sine	Cotangent	Tangent	Cosecant	Secant	Degree

Trigonometry Table

Degree	Sine	Cosine	Tangent	Cotangent	Secant	Cosecant	
37.5°	0.6088	0.7934	0.7673	1.3032	1.2605	1.6427	52.5°
38°	0.6157	0.788	0.7813	1.2799	1.269	1.6243	52°
38.5°	0.6225	0.7826	0.7954	1.2572	1.2778	1.6064	51.5°
39°	0.6293	0.7771	0.8098	1.2349	1.2868	1.589	51°
39.5°	0.6361	0.7716	0.8243	1.2131	1.296	1.5721	50.5°
40°	0.6428	0.766	0.8391	1.1918	1.3054	1.5557	50°
40.5°	0.6494	0.7604	0.8541	1.1708	1.3151	1.5398	49.5°
41°	0.6561	0.7547	0.8693	1.1504	1.325	1.5243	49°
41.5°	0.6626	0.749	0.8847	1.1303	1.3352	1.5092	48.5°
42°	0.6691	0.7431	0.9004	1.1106	1.3456	1.4945	48°
42.5°	0.6756	0.7373	0.9163	1.0913	1.3563	1.4802	47.5°
43°	0.682	0.7314	0.9325	1.0724	1.3673	1.4663	47°
43.5°	0.6884	0.7254	0.949	1.0538	1.3786	1.4527	46.5°
44°	0.6947	0.7193	0.9657	1.0355	1.3902	1.4396	46°
44.5°	0.7009	0.7133	0.9827	1.0176	1.402	1.4267	45.5°
45°	0.7071	0.7071	1	1	1.4142	1.4142	45°
	Cosine	Sine	Cotangent	Tangent	Cosecant	Secant	Degree

56 Total Thermal Expansion of Piping Material in inches per 100' above 32° F

Temperature F°	Carbon & Carbon Moly Steel	Cast Iron	Copper	Brass & Bronze	Wrought Iron
32	0	0	0	0	0
100	0.5	0.5	0.8	0.8	0.5
150	0.8	0.8	1.4	1.4	0.9
200	1.2	1.2	2.0	2.0	1.3
250	1.7	1.5	2.7	2.6	1.7
300	2.0	1.9	3.3	3.2	2.2
350	2.5	2.3	4.0	3.9	2.6
400	2.9	2.7	4.7	4.6	3.1
450	3.4	3.1	5.3	5.2	3.6
500	3.8	3.5	6.0	5.9	4.1
550	4.3	3.9	6.7	6.5	4.6
600	4.8	4.4	7.4	7.2	5.2
650	5.3	4.8	8.2	7.9	5.6
700	5.9	5.3	9.0	8.5	6.1
750	6.4	5.8	—	—	6.7
800	7.0	6.3	—	—	7.2
850	7.4	—	—	—	—
900	8.0	—	—	—	—
950	8.5	—	—	—	—
1000	9.1	—	—	—	—

Pattern Layout, Laterals, Any Angle

Draw full scale layout of header and lateral at the desired angle, as shown on Figure 22. The ordinates required to make a pattern for the lateral can be taken from this full scale layout.

The ordinate lengths are from the baseline shown on the lateral, to the points 1, 2, 3, 4. 5, 6, 7, 8, & 9, which are established by the intersection of the projection lines on the lateral and on the header.

Using these ordinate lengths, layout pattern as shown in Figure 23. Draw baseline which is equal to the outside circumference of the lateral from point 1 to point 1. Divide baseline into 16 equal spaces. Number as shown to correspond to numbering in Figure 22. (Get circumference and spacing from Pipe Circumference Table VI, pages 31 & 32.) Draw perpendicular lines to baseline at each space. Mark on perpendicular lines the ordinate lengths from Figure 22 full scale layout. Draw line connecting the ordinates free hand and cut out pattern on this line. Leave extra band of pattern material along bottom of pattern for ease of handling, as shown in Figure 23.

59

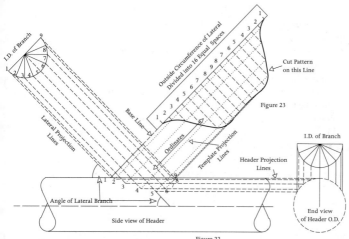

I.D. of Branch

9
8
7
6
1 2 3 4 5

Outside Circumference of Lateral
Divided into 16 Equal Spaces

1
2
3
4
5
6
7
8
9

1 2 3 4 5 6 7 8 9

Cut Pattern
on this Line

Figure 23

Base Line

Ordinates

Template Projection
Lines

Lateral Projection
Lines

Header Projection
Lines

I.D. of Branch

1
2
3
4 5 6 7 8 9

Angle of Lateral Branch

Side view of Header

End view
of Header O.D.

Figure 22

Pattern Layout For Mitred Turns

Draw full scale circumference (end view) of pipe. See Figure 24. Divide half of circumference into 8 equal parts. Number as shown in Figure 24. Draw side view of pipe on same centerline. Draw baseline "B" and cutline "A" at the desired pattern angle "PA". Draw projection lines from each numbered point on circumference and cross both "A" and "B" lines. Number as shown in Figure 24. The ordinates for the pattern are the lines between cutline "A" and baseline "B". Using these ordinates, layout pattern as shown in Figure 25.

Draw baseline "B" equal to circumference of pipe from point 1 to point 1. Divide "B" into 16 equal spaces. (Get circumference of pipe and ordinate spacing from Table VI, pages 31 and 32.) Number as shown in Figure 25. Draw perpendicular lines to baseline "B" at each space. Mark on perpendicular lines ordinate lengths from side view in Figure 24. Draw cut line "A" freehand and cut out pattern on this line. Leave extra band of pattern material on bottom of pattern for ease of handling. Mark size of pipe and angle of turn on pattern for identification.

61

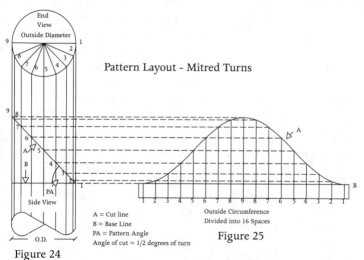

End
View
Outside Diameter

9   1
8   2
7   3
6   5   4

Pattern Layout - Mitred Turns

9
8
7
6
5
A
B
4
3
PA
1
Side View

O.D.

Figure 24

A = Cut line
B = Base Line
PA = Pattern Angle
Angle of cut = 1/2 degrees of turn

A

B

1 2 3 4 5 6 7 8 9 8 7 6 5 4 3 2 1

Outside Circumference
Divided into 16 Spaces

Figure 25

Pattern Layout—90 Degree Branch

Draw full scale end views of inside circumference of branch and outside circumference of header as shown in Figure 26. (Inside of branch must fit outside of header. See page 24, Figs. 13 & 14.) Divide half of branch circumference into 8 equal parts. Number as shown. Draw projection lines from these space marks, crossing base line and header circumference as shown in Figure 26. That portion of the projection lines between base line and header circumference are the ordinates for construction of the pattern as shown in Figure 27.

Draw base line in Figure 27 equal to outside circumference of branch from point 1 to point 1. Divide baseline into 16 equal parts. Erect perpendicular lines at each space mark on base line. Number as shown. Mark ordinate lengths on perpendicular lines, taken from Figure 26. Connect these points freehand and cut out pattern on this line. Mark pipe sizes on pattern for future reference.

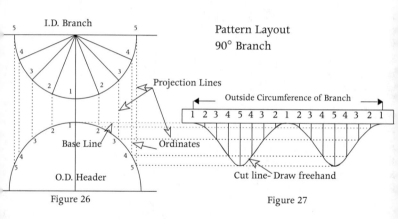

I.D. Branch

Pattern Layout
90° Branch

Projection Lines

Base Line

Ordinates

O.D. Header

Outside Circumference of Branch

Cut line- Draw freehand

Figure 26

Figure 27

U-Bolts all dimensions in Inches

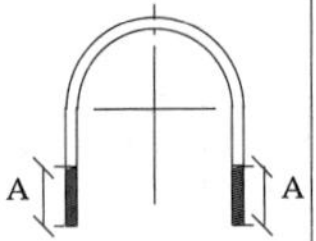

U-Bolt
Figure 28

NPS	Length 1/4 Rod	Length 3/8 Rod	Length 1/2 Rod	Length 5/8 Rod	Length 3/4 Rod	Thread "A"
1/4	3					3/4
3/8	3 1/4					7/8
1/2	4 1/4	4 1/2				7/8
3/4	4 3/4	5 1/2				7/8
1	5 1/2	5 3/4				7/8
1 1/4		6 3/4	7			1
1 1/2		7 1/4	7 1/2			1
2		8 3/4	9 1/2			1 1/4
2 1/2		10 1/4	10 3/4	11 1/4		1 1/4
3		12 1/2	12 3/4	13		1 1/4
4		14 1/2	15 1/4	16 1/2		1 1/2
5			17 1/2	18 1/2		2
6			21 1/2	22		2 1/2
8			26	27	28	2 1/2
10				33	34	2 1/2
12					38 1/2	2 1/2

2-Bolt Pipe Clamps (Inches)

NPS	Iron Size	Length	A	B	Hole Dia	Bolt Dia
$\frac{1}{2}$	$\frac{1}{8}$ x 1	3	1	$\frac{1}{2}$	$\frac{3}{8}$	$\frac{1}{4}$
$\frac{3}{4}$	$\frac{1}{8}$ x 1	$3\frac{1}{2}$	1	$\frac{1}{2}$	$\frac{3}{8}$	$\frac{1}{4}$
1	$\frac{1}{4}$ x $1\frac{1}{4}$	$4\frac{1}{2}$	$1\frac{1}{4}$	$\frac{5}{8}$	$\frac{1}{2}$	$\frac{3}{8}$
$1\frac{1}{4}$	$\frac{1}{4}$ x $1\frac{1}{4}$	5	$1\frac{1}{4}$	$\frac{5}{8}$	$\frac{1}{2}$	$\frac{3}{8}$
$1\frac{1}{2}$	$\frac{1}{4}$ x $1\frac{1}{4}$	6	$1\frac{1}{2}$	$\frac{3}{4}$	$\frac{1}{2}$	$\frac{3}{8}$
2	$\frac{1}{4}$ x $1\frac{1}{2}$	$6\frac{3}{4}$	$1\frac{1}{2}$	$\frac{3}{4}$	$\frac{5}{8}$	$\frac{1}{2}$
$2\frac{1}{2}$	$\frac{1}{4}$ x $1\frac{1}{2}$	$7\frac{1}{2}$	$1\frac{1}{2}$	$\frac{3}{4}$	$\frac{5}{8}$	$\frac{1}{2}$
3	$\frac{3}{8}$ x 2	$9\frac{1}{2}$	2	1	$\frac{3}{4}$	$\frac{5}{8}$
4	$\frac{3}{8}$ x 2	10	2	1	$\frac{3}{4}$	$\frac{5}{8}$
5	$\frac{3}{8}$ x $2\frac{1}{2}$	$12\frac{1}{2}$	$2\frac{1}{2}$	$1\frac{1}{4}$	$\frac{3}{4}$	$\frac{5}{8}$
6	$\frac{3}{8}$ x $2\frac{1}{2}$	14	$2\frac{1}{2}$	$1\frac{1}{4}$	$\frac{7}{8}$	$\frac{3}{4}$
8	$\frac{3}{8}$ x $2\frac{1}{2}$	17	$2\frac{1}{2}$	$1\frac{1}{4}$	$\frac{7}{8}$	$\frac{3}{4}$
10	$\frac{1}{2}$ x 3	$21\frac{1}{2}$	3	$1\frac{1}{2}$	1	$\frac{7}{8}$
12	$\frac{1}{2}$ x 3	$25\frac{1}{2}$	3	$1\frac{1}{2}$	1	$\frac{7}{8}$
14	$\frac{1}{2}$ x $3\frac{1}{2}$	$27\frac{1}{2}$	$3\frac{1}{2}$	$1\frac{3}{4}$	1	$\frac{7}{8}$
16	$\frac{1}{2}$ x $3\frac{1}{2}$	31	$3\frac{1}{2}$	$1\frac{3}{4}$	1	$\frac{7}{8}$
18	$\frac{1}{2}$ x $3\frac{1}{2}$	34	$3\frac{1}{2}$	$1\frac{3}{4}$	$1\frac{1}{8}$	1
20	$\frac{3}{4}$ x 4	38	4	2	$1\frac{1}{4}$	$1\frac{1}{8}$
24	$\frac{3}{4}$ x 4	$43\frac{1}{2}$	4	2	$1\frac{3}{8}$	$1\frac{1}{4}$
30	$\frac{3}{4}$ x 4	$54\frac{1}{2}$	4	2	$1\frac{1}{2}$	$1\frac{3}{8}$

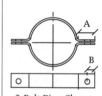

2-Bolt Pipe Clamp

Figure 29

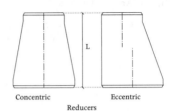

Concentric   Eccentric

Reducers

Butt Weld Fittings

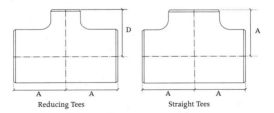

Reducing Tees   Straight Tees

NPS	Outlet	A	D	L
1	1	1½	—	
1	¾	1½	1½	2
1	½	1½	1½	2
1¼	1¼	1⅞		
1¼	1	1⅞	1⅞	2
1¼	¾	1⅞	1⅞	2
1¼	½	1⅞	1⅞	2
1½	1½	2¼	—	
1½	1¼	2¼	2¼	2½
1½	1	2¼	2¼	2½
1½	¾	2¼	2¼	2½
1½	½	2¼	2¼	2½
2	2	2½	—	
2	1½	2½	2⅜	3
2	1¼	2½	2¼	3
2	1	2½	2	3
2	¾	2½	1¾	3
2½	2½	3	—	
2½	2	3	2¾	3½

NPS	Outlet	A	D	L
2½	1½	3	2⅝	3½
2½	1¼	3	2½	3½
2½	1	3	2¼	3½
3	3	3⅜	—	
3	2½	3⅜	3¼	3½
3	2	3⅜	3	3½
3	1½	3⅜	2⅞	3½
3	1¼	3⅜	2¾	3½
3½	3½	3¾	—	
3½	3	3¾	3⅝	4
3½	2½	3¾	3½	4
3½	2	3¾	3¼	4
3½	1½	3¾	3⅛	4
4	4	4⅛	—	
4	3½	4⅛	4	4
4	3	4⅛	3⅞	4
4	2½	4⅛	3¾	4
4	2	4⅛	3½	4
4	1½	4⅛	3⅜	4

Straight Tees—Reducing Tees—Concentric and Eccentric Reducers

NPS	Outlet	A	D	L
5	5	$4\frac{7}{8}$	—	—
5	$3\frac{1}{2}$	$4\frac{7}{8}$	$4\frac{1}{2}$	5
5	4	$4\frac{7}{8}$	$4\frac{5}{8}$	5
5	3	$4\frac{7}{8}$	$4\frac{3}{8}$	5
5	$2\frac{1}{2}$	$4\frac{7}{4}$	$4\frac{1}{4}$	5
5	2	$4\frac{7}{8}$	$4\frac{1}{8}$	5
6	6	$5\frac{5}{8}$	—	—
6	5	$5\frac{5}{8}$	$5\frac{3}{8}$	$5\frac{1}{2}$
6	4	$5\frac{5}{8}$	$5\frac{1}{8}$	$5\frac{1}{2}$
6	$3\frac{1}{2}$	$5\frac{5}{8}$	5	$5\frac{1}{2}$
6	3	$5\frac{5}{8}$	$4\frac{7}{8}$	$5\frac{1}{2}$
6	$2\frac{1}{2}$	$5\frac{5}{8}$	$4\frac{3}{4}$	$5\frac{1}{2}$
8	8	7	—	—
8	6	7	$6\frac{5}{8}$	6
8	5	7	$6\frac{3}{8}$	6
8	4	6	$7\frac{1}{8}$	6
8	$3\frac{1}{2}$	7	6	6
10	10	$8\frac{1}{2}$	—	—
10	8	$8\frac{1}{2}$	8	7

NPS	Outlet	A	D	L
10	6	$8\frac{1}{2}$	$7\frac{5}{8}$	7
10	5	$8\frac{1}{2}$	$7\frac{1}{2}$	7
10	4	$8\frac{1}{2}$	$7\frac{1}{4}$	7
12	12	10	—	—
12	10	10	$9\frac{1}{2}$	8
12	8	10	9	8
12	6	10	$8\frac{5}{8}$	8
12	5	10	$8\frac{1}{2}$	8
14	14	11	—	—
14	12	11	$10\frac{5}{8}$	13
14	10	11	$10\frac{1}{8}$	13
14	8	11	$9\frac{3}{4}$	13
14	6	11	$9\frac{3}{8}$	13
16	16	12	—	—
16	14	12	12	14
16	12	12	$11\frac{5}{8}$	14
16	10	12	$11\frac{1}{8}$	14
16	8	12	$10\frac{3}{4}$	14
16	6	12	$10\frac{3}{8}$	14

NPS	Outlet	A	D	L
18	18	$13\frac{1}{2}$	—	—
18	16	$13\frac{1}{2}$	13	15
18	14	$13\frac{1}{2}$	13	15
18	12	$13\frac{1}{2}$	$12\frac{5}{8}$	15
18	10	$13\frac{1}{2}$	$12\frac{1}{8}$	15
18	8	$13\frac{1}{2}$	$11\frac{3}{4}$	15
20	20	15	—	—
20	18	15	$14\frac{1}{2}$	20
20	16	15	14	20
20	14	15	14	20
20	12	15	$13\frac{5}{8}$	20
20	10	15	$13\frac{1}{8}$	20
20	8	15	$12\frac{3}{4}$	20
24	24	17	—	—
24	20	17	17	20
24	18	17	$16\frac{1}{2}$	20
24	16	17	16	20
24	14	17	16	20
24	12	17	$15\frac{5}{8}$	20
24	10	17	$15\frac{1}{8}$	20

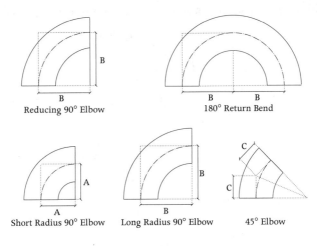

Reducing 90° Elbow

180° Return Bend

Short Radius 90° Elbow

Long Radius 90° Elbow

45° Elbow

	Dimensions in Inches, Center to End		
NPS	A	B	C
1	1	$1\frac{1}{2}$	$\frac{7}{8}$
$1\frac{1}{4}$	$1\frac{1}{4}$	$1\frac{7}{8}$	1
$1\frac{1}{2}$	$1\frac{1}{2}$	$2\frac{1}{4}$	$1\frac{1}{8}$
2	2	3	$1\frac{3}{8}$
$2\frac{1}{2}$	$2\frac{1}{2}$	$3\frac{3}{4}$	$1\frac{3}{4}$
3	3	$4\frac{1}{2}$	2
$3\frac{1}{2}$	$3\frac{1}{2}$	$5\frac{1}{4}$	$2\frac{1}{4}$
4	4	6	$2\frac{1}{2}$
5	5	$7\frac{1}{2}$	$3\frac{1}{8}$
6	6	9	$3\frac{3}{4}$
8	8	12	5
10	10	15	$6\frac{1}{4}$
12	12	18	$7\frac{1}{2}$
14	14	21	$8\frac{3}{4}$
16	16	24	10
18	18	27	$11\frac{1}{4}$
20	20	30	$12\frac{1}{2}$
24	24	36	15

72

Weld Neck Flanges

See Pages 38 through 43 for other flange dimensions.

Flg Size	150 lb. Length through hub Y	300 lb. Length through hub Y
1/2	1 7/8	2 1/16
3/4	2 1/16	2 1/4
1	2 3/16	2 7/16
1 1/4	2 1/4	2 9/16
1 1/2	2 7/16	2 11/16
2	2 1/2	2 3/4
2 1/2	2 3/4	3
3	2 3/4	3 1/8
3 1/2	2 13/16	3 3/16
4	3	3 3/8
5	3 1/2	3 7/8
6	3 1/2	3 7/8
8	4	4 3/8
10	4	4 5/8
12	4 1/2	5 1/8
14	5	5 5/8
16	5	5 3/4
18	5 1/2	6 1/4
20	5 11/16	6 3/8
24	6	6 5/8

Metric Symbols

in	=	inches	pt	=	pints
ft	=	feet	qt	=	quarts
yd	=	yards	gal	=	gallons
mi	=	miles	cu	=	cubic
cm	=	centimeters	F	=	fahrenheit
m	=	meters	C	=	celcius
km	=	kilometers	g	=	grams
sq	=	square	kg	=	kilogram
ha	=	hectares	mm	=	millimeters
oz	=	ounces	l	=	liters
lb	=	pounds			
t	=	tons			

Metric Conversion Factors
Approximate

To Metric

Length
in x 2.5 = cm
ft x 30 = cm
yd x 0.9 = m
mi x 1.6 = km

Area
sq in x 6.5 = sq cm
sq ft. x 0.09 = sq m
sq yd x 0.8 = sq m
sq mi x 2.6 = sq km
Acres x 0.4 = ha

Mass (weight)
oz. x 28 = g
lb x 0.45 = kg
Short tons x 0.9 = t

Volume
pt x 0.47 = l
qt x 0.95 = l
gal x 3.8 = l
cu ft x 0.03 = cu m
cu yd x 0.76 = cu m

Temperature (exact)
°F x 5/9* = °C
(*after subtracting 32)

From Metric

Length
mm x 0.04 = in
cm x 0.4 = in
m x 3.3 = ft
m x 1.1 = yd
km x 0.6 = mi

Area
Sq. cm x .16 = sq. in
sq.m x 1.2 = sq yd
sq. km x 0.4 = sq mi
ha x 2.5 = acres

Mass (weight)
g x 0.035 = oz
kg x 2.2 = lb
t x 1.1 = short tons

Volume
l x 2.1 = pt
l x 1.06 = qt
l x 0.26 = gal
cu. m x 35 = cu ft
cu. m x 1.3 = cu yd

Temperature (exact)
°C x 9/5* = °F
(*then add 32)

For more information on pipefitting books and tools, please go to

http://www.pipefitter.com

or
call 800-462-6487.